New York Yankees
Trivia Quiz Book

500 Questions on the Bronx Bombers

Chris Bradshaw

ISBN-13: 978-1-9161230-3-8

Front cover image created by headfuzz by grimboid. Check out his great collection of TV, movie and sport-themed posters online at:

https://www.etsy.com/shop/headfuzzbygrimboid

Introduction

Think you know about the New York Yankees? Put your knowledge to the test with this selection of quizzes on the Bronx Bombers.

The book covers the whole history of the club, from the Babe Ruth era and the record breakers of the 1950s through to the 1970s glory years and the dominant teams of the 1990s, right up to the present day.

The biggest names in Yankees history are present and correct so look out for questions on Derek Jeter, Mariano Rivera, Joe DiMaggio, Aaron Judge, Lou Gehrig, Bernie Williams and many, many more.

There are 500 questions in all covering pitchers and catchers, coaches and closers, sluggers and stealers and much else besides.

Each quiz contains 20 questions and is either a mixed bag of pot luck testers or is centered on a specific category such as Pitchers or the 2009 World Champions.

There are easy, medium and hard questions, offering something for New York novices as well as professors of Yankees history.

You'll find the answers to each quiz below the bottom of the following quiz. For example, the answers to Quiz 1: Pot Luck, are underneath Quiz 2: Pitchers. The only exception is Quiz 25: Pot Luck. The answers to these can be found under the Quiz 1 questions.

All statistics relate to the regular season only unless otherwise stated are accurate up to the close of the 2019 season.

We hope you enjoy the New York Yankees Trivia Quiz Book.

About the Author

Chris Bradshaw has written over 20 quiz books including titles for Britain's biggest selling daily newspaper, The Sun, and The Times (of London). In addition to baseball, he has written extensively on the NFL, soccer, cricket, darts and poker.

He lives in Birmingham, England and has been following the Major League Baseball for over 30 years.

Acknowledgements

Many thanks to Ken and Veronica Bradshaw, Heidi Grant, Steph, James, Ben and Will Roe and Graham Nash.

CONTENTS

Quiz 1: Pot Luck

1. The Yankees are based in which of New York's five boroughs?

2. Who was appointed the team's manager in December 2017?

3. Which star's #2 jersey was retired on May 14, 2017?

4. Which Yankees great was the first player to be unanimously voted into the Baseball Hall of Fame?

5. Which pitcher, who spent 15 seasons with the Yankees, holds the MLB record for the most career postseason wins with 19?

6. Which two Yankees both hit home runs in their first Major League at-bats in an August 2016 game against the Rays?

7. The Yankees' #1 jersey number is retired in honor of which player and manager?

8. True or false – The Yankees have never finished bottom of the AL East?

9. Which 40-year-old, pinch hitting for Alex Rodriguez, hit two home runs in Game 3 of the 2012 ALDS against Baltimore?

10. In Game 3 of the 2018 ALDS against Boston, who became just the second position player in MLB history to take to the mound in a postseason game?

11. 'Holy Cow!' is a phrase commonly associated with which shortstop turned broadcaster?

12. Which multiple World Series-winner is also an accomplished guitarist who has been nominated for a Latin Grammy award?

13. The 2019 Yankees set a Major League record after hitting at least one home run in how many consecutive games?

14. Which Yankee was the author of a 2019 autobiography called 'Full Count: The Education of a Pitcher'?

15. In 2019, the Yankees played two regular season games in which overseas city?

16. Which team did they face in that series?

17. Since its creation in 1983, who are the two Yankees to have won the AL Manager of the Year Award?

18. Why is graphic artist Henry Alonzo Keller an important part of the history of the Yankees?

19. Which legendary Yankee appeared in a 1938 movie western called 'Rawhide'? a) Bill Dickey b) Lou Gehrig c) Babe Ruth

20. By what name were the Yankees formerly known? a) New York Highlanders b) New York Lowlanders c) New York Midlanders

Quiz 25: Answers

1. 'Enter Sandman' 2. Miguel Andújar 3. Bobby Bonds 4. Reggie Jackson 5. L.A. Dodgers 6. Aaron Judge 7. Yogi Berra 8. David John 9. Mel Stottlemyre 10. Goose Gossage 11. Whitey Ford 12. Babe Ruth 13. Bernie Williams 14. Derek Jeter 15. Gary Cooper 16. Don Mattingly 17. The House that Ruth Built 18. Brian Cashman 19. b) Mariekson 20. b) 42

Quiz 2: Pitchers

1. Who is the only player to have pitched in over 1,000 games for the Yankees?

2. Whose 236 career wins are the most by a Yankees pitcher?

3. Which right-hander tied an American League record in 2001 after winning 16 straight games?

4. 'El Duque' was the nickname of which Yankees pitcher?

5. Who is the only Yankees pitcher with more than 2,000 career strikeouts?

6. Which Yankees pitcher was nicknamed 'Louisiana Lightning'?

7. Which New York pitcher won Gold Glove honors in 2001, 2003 and 2008?

8. Who is the only pitcher drafted by the Yankees to amass 200 career Major League wins?

9. In 1975, who became the last Yankee to pitch 30 complete games in a single season?

10. Which Yankees right-hander tossed a perfect game in a 1999 contest against the Expos?

11. Which left-hander pitched a perfect game against the Twins in May 1998?

12. Which starting pitcher recorded the clinching win in the 2009 ALDS, ALCS and World Series?

13. Of Yankees pitchers with over 800 innings pitched, who has the best ERA?

14. Which Red Sox pitcher struck out a record 19 Yankees batters in a September 1999 game?

15. Who is the only Yankees pitcher to throw more than one no-hitter?

16. Who are the two right-handed Yankees pitchers have won the Cy Young Award?

17. Who are the three left-handed Yankees pitchers to have won the Cy Young Award?

18. Before signing with the Yankees, CC Sabathia enjoyed a short spell with which National League club?

19. Between 1998 and 2000 Mariano Rivera pitched how many postseason innings without giving up a run? a) 31.1 b) 32.1 c) 33.1

20. Mariano Rivera set the team record for the most saves in a single season in 2004 with how many? a) 52 b) 53 c) 54

Quiz 1: Answers

1.The Bronx 2. Aaron Boone 3. Derek Jeter 4. Mariano Rivera 5. Andy Pettitte 6. Tyler Austin and Aaron Judge 7. Billy Martin 8. True 9. Raul Ibanez 10. Austin Romine 11. Phil Rizzuto 12. Bernie Williams 13. 31 games 14. David Cone 15. London 16. Boston 17. Buck Showalter and Joe Torre 18. He designed the team's famous Top Hat logo 19. b) Lou Gehrig 20. a) New York Highlanders

Quiz 3: Pot Luck

1. Which Yankee hit three home runs and drove in 10 runs in a 2005 game against the Angels?

2. Who is the only Yankee to have had his jersey number retired who didn't win a World Series with the club?

3. Who hit more than 30 home runs and stole more than 30 bases in both the 2002 and 2003 seasons?

4. In 2017, Aaron Judge set the MLB record for the most home runs by a rookie. Whose record did he break?

5. Which Yankee appeared on 10 World Series-winning teams, the most by any player in Major League Baseball history?

6. True or false – The Yankees have won more American League pennants than any other team?

7. What is Goose Gossage's real first name?

8. In what Florida city do the Yankees play home Spring Training games?

9. Which Yankees pitcher threw a perfect game in Game 5 of the 1956 World Series?

10. Which Yankee was the last player in Major League Baseball to wear the #42 jersey which has been retired in honor of Jackie Robinson?

11. True or false – The Yankees lost the first two games of the 1996 World Series by a combined score of 16-1?

12. The Yankees have recorded more wins in franchise history over which opponent than any other?

13. Which Yankees great holds the MLB record for the most RBIs in postseason play?

14. In April 2012, the Yankees famously overturned a 9-0 deficit to beat which club by a score of 15-9?

15. Filling in at shortstop for Derek Jeter against the White Sox on August 2, 2007, who marked his first at-bat as a Yankee by hitting a three-run homer?

16. Which Yankees pitcher was named the AL Comeback Player of the Year for 2013?

17. Babe Ruth was sold from the Red Sox to the Yankees in order to finance which Broadway musical?

18. Since its creation in 1973, who is the only Yankee to have won the Edgar Martinez Award for the game's top designated hitter?

19. What was Yogi Berra's real first name? a) Lawrence b) Leonard c) Lionel

20. What was the name of the Yankees' mascot from the late 1970s and early 1980s? a) Andy b) Dandy c) Randy

Quiz 2: Answers

1. Mariano Rivera 2. Whitey Ford 3. Roger Clemens 4. Orlando Hernandez 5. Andy Pettitte 6. Ron Guidry 7. Mike Mussina 8. Andy Pettitte 9. Catfish Hunter 10. David Cone 11. David Wells 12. Andy Pettitte 13. Mariano Rivera 14. Pedro Martinez 15. Allie Reynolds 16. Bob Turley and Roger Clemens 17. Whitey Ford, Sparky Lyle and Ron Guidry 18. Milwaukee Brewers 19. c) 33.1 IP 20. c) 54

Quiz 4: Batters

1. Who holds the team record for the most home runs in a single season?

2. How many home runs did he hit to set that record?

3. Whose 238 hits in 1986 are the most by a Yankees batter in a single season?

4. Who is the Yankees' all-time leader in home runs?

5. Derek Jeter is the all-time leader in At Bats for the Yankees. Who is second on that list?

6. Who holds the record for the most home runs in a single season by a Yankees catcher?

7. In 2002, who set the franchise record for the most hits in a single season by a switch hitter?

8. Which Yankee led the AL in home runs in 2017 after going yard 52 times?

9. In 2009, two Yankees batters both registered 200 hits. Which two?

10. Which Yankee led the AL in RBIs in 2011 with 119?

11. Which switch-hitting outfielder hit for the cycle in a 2009 game against the White Sox?

12. In July 2018, who became the third Yankee to hit three home runs in a game against the Red Sox?

13. Who also hit a hat-trick of home runs in a May 2010 game against the Red Sox at Fenway Park?

14. In a 1972 game at Detroit, Lindy McDaniel became the last Yankee to do what?

15. Who holds the franchise record for the most home runs in a single season by a switch hitter?

16. Who hit two home runs in his debut appearance for the Yankees against Toronto in March 2018?

17. In 2010, which catcher became the first Yankee in over 70 years to hit grand slams in consecutive games?

18. Who holds the team record for the most leadoff home runs in a single season?

19. The 2018 Yankees set a franchise record after hitting how many home runs? a) 267 b) 277 c) 287

20. Joe DiMaggio's record 1941 hitting streak ran for how many games? a) 55 b) 56 c) 57

Quiz 3: Answers

1. Alex Rodriguez 2. Don Mattingly 3. Alfonso Soriano 4. Mark McGwire 5. Yogi Berra 6. True 7. Rich 8. Tampa 9. Don Larsen 10. Mariano Rivera 11. True 12. Baltimore 13. Bernie Williams 14. Boston 15. Wilson Betemit 16. Mariano Rivera 17. No, No Nanette 18. Don Baylor 19. a) Lawrence 20. b) Dandy

Quiz 5: Pot Luck

1. The Yankees have more World Series wins than any other club. Which National League team is second on the most World Series wins list?

2. Which Yankees catcher was tragically killed in a plane crash on August 2, 1979?

3. Which team swept the Yankees in the 1976 World Series?

4. Which Yankee was named AL Rookie of the Year in 1996?

5. Which NFL superstar attended Yankees Spring Training in 2018?

6. What is the nickname of the vociferous fan group that occupies Section 203 of Yankee Stadium?

7. True or false – In a June 2019 game against the Mets, all nine Yankees starters scored a run?

8. Which Yankee was named MVP of the 2000 All-Star Game?

9. The award given to the AL Reliever of the Year is named after which Yankees great?

10. Which Yankees pitcher won the award in 2015?

11. Which Yankee won the MVP Award in the 2013 World Baseball Classic after helping the Dominican Republic to the title?

12. Which outfielder, who spent his 15th and final year in the big leagues with the Yankees, stole home base for the first time in his career in a September 2013 game against the White Sox?

13. Whose 141.0 innings pitched in the postseason are the most in MLB history?

14. The Yankees acquired Alex Rodriguez following a trade with which club?

15. Who holds the record for the most multiple home run-games in team history?

16. At 6ft 7in, which Yankee is the tallest player to play center fielder in MLB history?

17. Who is the Yankees' all-time leader in postseason home runs?

18. 'Gator: My Life in Pinstripes' was the title of the autobiography of which former Yankees star?

19. What is the real first name of former Yankees manager Stump Merrill? a) Carl b) Charles c) Chester

20. Lou Gehrig appeared in how many consecutive games for the Yankees? a) 2,120 b) 2,130 c) 2,140

Quiz 4: Answers

1. Roger Maris 2. 61 home runs 3. Don Mattingly 4. Babe Ruth 5. Micky Mantle 6. Gary Sanchez 7. Bernie Williams 8. Aaron Judge 9. Derek Jeter and Robinson Cano 10. Curtis Granderson 11. Melky Cabrera 12. Aaron Hicks 13. Mark Teixera 14. Pitcher to hit a home run 15. Micky Mantle 16. Giancarlo Stanton 17. Jorge Posada 18. Alfonso Soriano 19. a) 267 home runs 20. b) 56 games

Quiz 6: Ballparks

1. In what year did the Yankees play their first game at the new Yankee Stadium?

2. The Yankees were beaten 10-2 in the first game at the new Yankee Stadium by which team?

3. Who was the first batter to score a home run at the new Yankee Stadium?

4. The five best attended regular season games at the new Yankee Stadium were all against which opponent?

5. Who holds the record for the most hits at the old Yankee Stadium?

6. The last pitch thrown at the old Yankee Stadium was tossed by which legendary Yankee?

7. During the 1974 and 1975 seasons the Yankees played home games at which venue?

8. Which division rival did the Yankees defeat in the last game played at the original Yankee Stadium?

9. The Yankees were routed by a record score of 22-0 in an August 2004 game at Yankee Stadium against which team?

10. True or false – The New York Football Giants played home games at Yankee Stadium in the 1950s, 60s and 70s?

11. In 1961, the Yankees set a Major League record after winning how many home games?

12. In 2009, the Yankees set an unwanted club record after giving up 14 runs in a single inning in a home game against which team?

13. Between 1913 and 1922 the Yankees played home games at which famous venue?

14. What is the name of the public park that sits on the grounds of the former Yankee Stadium

15. The Yankees defeated which team 7-2 in the first playoff game hosted at the current Yankee Stadium?

16. What is the name of the stadium where the Yankees play their home Spring Training games?

17. In May 2019, which NL West team became the last club to make their first visit to the new Yankee Stadium?

18. What was the last song played over the public address system in the final game played at the original Yankee Stadium?

19. What was the name of the Yankees' first home? a) Hilltop Park b) Memorial Park c) State Park

20. What is the seating capacity of Yankee Stadium? a) 45,309 b) 46,309 c) 47,309

Quiz 5: Answers

1. St Louis Cardinals 2. Thurman Munson 3. Cincinnati 4. Derek Jeter 5. Russell Wilson 6. The Bleacher Creatures 7. True 8. Derek Jeter 9. Mariano Rivera 10. Andrew Miller 11. Robinson Cano 12. Vernon Wells 13. Mariano Rivera 14. Texas Rangers 15. Babe Ruth 16. Aaron Judge 17. Bernie Williams 18. Ron Guidry 19. a) Carl 20. b) 2,130 games

Quiz 7: Pot Luck

1. Who famously celebrated the 1996 World Series win by riding off the field on a police horse?

2. What is the official theme song of the Yankees?

3. Who holds the team record for the most home runs by a Yankees rookie?

4. The Yankees won back-to-back championships in 1977 and 1978, beating which team in the World Series both times?

5. Which Yankees catcher was behind the plate for no-hitters in 1996 and 1999?

6. Who hit his 600th home run in a 2010 game against Toronto at Yankee Stadium?

7. Who was the first Yankee to be inducted into the Hall of Fame?

8. Which Yankees pitcher was named the MVP of the 2013 All-Star Game?

9. Which Yankees great was briefly benched in 1991 after refusing to get his hair cut?

10. Who was the first Taiwanese-born player to play for the Yankees?

11. Which Yankees first baseman was suspended for four games for his involvement in a brawl with the Red Sox in April 2018?

12. Which Yankee was the first African-American to win the AL MVP Award?

13. The longest postseason drought in team history lasted how many years?

14. The Yankees have suffered more defeats at the hands of which opponent than any other?

15. How tall was Hall of Famer 'Wee' Willie Keeler, the shortest player to wear Yankees pinstripes?

16. In the second round of the 1981 MLB Draft the Yankees selected which future Hall of Fame NFL quarterback?

17. Which Yankee was named the MVP of the 1973 and 1977 World Series?

18. Which DH tied a franchise record in an April 2017 game against Baltimore after walking five times?

19. What was the nickname of the dominant 1920s Yankees line-up? a) Murderers' Column b) Murderers' Row c) Murderers' Yard

20. During the 1990s and 2000s the Yankees reached the postseason in how many consecutive years? a) 12 b) 13 c) 14

Quiz 6: Answers

1. 2009 2. Cleveland 3. Jorge Posada 4. Boston 5. Derek Jeter 6. Mariano Rivera 7. Shea Stadium 8. Baltimore 9. Cleveland 10. True 11. 65 games 12. Cleveland 13. The Polo Grounds 14. Heritage Fields 15. Minnesota 16. George Steinbrenner Stadium 17. San Diego 18. 'New York, New York' by Frank Sinatra 19. a) Hilltop Park 20. c) 47,309

Quiz 8: 2009 World Champions

1. Which team did the Yankees defeat in the 2009 World Series?

2. What was the Series score?

3. Who was named the 2009 World Series MVP?

4. The Yankees started their 2009 postseason run by defeating which opponent in the ALDS?

5. They followed that by beating which team in the ALCS?

6. Who hit a grand slam and a 3-run homer in the same inning in the regular season finale against Tampa Bay?

7. Who was the manager of the all-conquering 2009 Yankees team?

8. Who led the team in home runs in 2009, smashing 39 of them during the regular season?

9. True or false – The Yankees were 0-8 in their first 8 meetings against Boston during the 2009 season?

10. Which infielder missed just a single game throughout the whole of the 2009 season?

11. Whose 19 wins were the most by a Yankees pitcher during the 2009 regular season?

12. Who was the only Yankees pitcher to win All-Star honors in 2009?

13. Which two non-pitching Yankees were also named All Stars?

14. True of False – Pitcher Andy Pettitte became the oldest player in Major League history to win the clinching game of a World Series?

15. CC Sabathia and Andy Pettitte were two of the four Yankees pitchers to start more than 30 games in 2009. Who were the other two?

16. Which leftfielder from the 2009 team later went on to represent Thailand in the World Baseball Classic?

17. In August 2009, who became the first Yankee to hit for the cycle in 14 years in a game against the White Sox?

18. Which switch-hitter led the team in walks in 2009 with 97?

19. How many games did the Yankees win during the 2009 regular season? a) 102 b) 103 c) 104

20. The Yankees set a Major League record in 2009 after going errorless in how many consecutive games? a) 16 b) 17 c) 18

Quiz 7: Answers

1. Wade Boggs 2. Here Come the Yankees 3. Aaron Judge 4. L.A. Dodgers 5. Joe Girardi 6. Alex Rodriguez 7. Babe Ruth 8. Mariano Rivera 9. Don Mattingly 10. Chien-Ming Wang 11. Tyler Austin 12. Elston Howard 13. 18 years 14. Boston 15. 5ft 4in 16. John Elway 17. Reggie Jackson 18. Matt Holliday 19. b) Murderers' Row 20. b) 13

Quiz 9: Pot Luck

1. Who hit a famous 10th inning walk-off homer in Game 1 of the 1999 ALCS against the Red Sox?

2. Whose 15 appearances in the All-Star game are the most by a Yankees player?

3. What number jersey, which has subsequently been retired, did catcher Jorge Posada wear?

4. Which Yankees batter struck 10 home runs during a prolific eight game-stretch during the 1987 season?

5. What do the letters CC stand for in the name CC Sabathia?

6. Only one franchise has more World Series losses than the Yankees. Which one?

7. Whose 25 wins and ERA of 1.74 made him a unanimous choice for the AL Cy Young Award in 1978?

8. True or false – The Yankees were the first team to reach the American League playoffs as a 'wild card'?

9. Which Yankee won the AL Rookie of the Year Award in 1970?

10. Who hit a home run in his first Major League at bat in a September 2004 game against the Red Sox at Fenway Park?

11. In between spells with the Yankees, pitcher Andy Pettitte spent three seasons with which club?

12. Which Yankees great was the owner of a successful thoroughbred racehorse called Game On Dude?

13. Which Yankee was awarded the Presidential Medal of Freedom by President Donald Trump in September 2019?

14. Whose number 4 jersey was the first to be retired in the history of Major League Baseball?

15. Up to and including the 2019 season, the Yankees had a winning record against every Major League club bar one. Which one?

16. Which leadoff hitter, who enjoyed three successful seasons in Pinstripes in the mid-1970s, was known as 'Mick the Quick'?

17. Harry Hanson, the youngest player to play for the Yankees, was how old when he made his debut?

18. In August 2006, the Yankees were involved in the longest nine-inning game in MLB history. Who was their opponent?

19. How long did that marathon matchup last? a) 4 hours 25 mins b) 4 hours 35 mins c) 4 hours 45 mins

20. What is the nickname of the Yankees' Triple-A affiliate that plays in Scranton/Wilkes-Barre? a) RailRiders b) RangeRiders c) RoughRiders

Quiz 8: Answers

1. Philadelphia Phillies 2. Yankees 4-2 Phillies 3. Hideki Matsui 4. Minnesota 5. L.A. Angels of Anaheim 6. Alex Rodriguez 7. Joe Girardi 8. Mark Teixeira 9. True 10. Robinson Cano 11. CC Sabathia 12. Mariano Rivera 13. Derek Jeter and Mark Teixeira 14. False 15. A.J. Burnett and Joba Chamberlain 16. Johnny Damon 17. Melky Cabrera 18. Nick Swisher 19. b) 103 20. c) 18 games

Quiz 10: Derek Jeter

1. In what year did Jeter make his Major League debut?

2. Jeter struck his first career home run off which veteran Nicaraguan pitcher?

3. In which round of the 1992 MLB Draft did the Yankees select Jeter?

4. Jeter's MLB career ran for how many years?

5. Jeter hit the first pitch of Game 4 of the 2000 World Series for a home run off which Mets pitcher?

6. Jeter holds the record for the most hits in Yankees' history. Whose record did he break?

7. How many times was Jeter voted to the All-Star Game in his stellar career?

8. On 9 July 2011, Jeter became just the second player in MLB history to reach his 3,000th hit with a home run, emulating which former Yankee?

9. Jeter recorded his 3,000th hit in a game against which division rival?

10. Out of a possible 397 votes to secure his entry into the Baseball Hall of Fame, Jeter received how many?

11. How many World Series rings did Jeter win throughout his career?

12. Jeter gained his 'Mr. November' nickname after hitting a game-winning home run off which Arizona pitcher in Game 4 of the 2001 World Series?

13. How many Gold Gloves did Jeter win?

14. Jeter ended up bloodied after famously diving into the crowd to catch a foul ball in a famous 2004 game against which club?

15. In 2017, Jeter became a part owner of which MLB franchise?

16. Growing up, which Yankees outfielder was Jeter's favorite player?

17. True or false – Jeter hit a walk-off single in his final game at Yankee Stadium?

18. Jeter hit more home runs at which opposition ballpark than any other?

19. What is Jeter's middle name? a) Granderson b) Henderson c) Sanderson

20. What was Jeter's final career batting average? a) .300 b) .305 c) .310

Quiz 9: Answers

1. Bernie Williams 2. Mickey Mantle 3. #20 4. Don Mattingly 5. Carsten Charles 6. The Dodgers 7. Ron Guidry 8. True 9. Thurmon Munson 10. Andy Phillips 11. Houston 12. Joe Torre 13. Mariano Rivera 14. Lou Gehrig 15. Miami Marlins 16. Mickey Rivers 17. 17 years old 18. Boston 19. c) 4 hours 45 mins 20. a) RailRiders

Quiz 11: Pot Luck

1. Which Yankees pitcher threw a no-hitter in a May 1996 game against the Mariners?

2. Which Yankee finished second in the ballot for the 2016 AL Rookie of the Year despite appearing in just 53 games?

3. Which position player retired three batters in a single inning of relief pitching against the Rays in April 2009?

4. The Yankees reached the World Series how many times during the 1980s?

5. Which Yankees first baseman hit a home run in his first Major League at bat in September 1966. He also hit a home run in his final Major League at bat while with the Dodgers in 1969?

6. Which former Yankee launched aftershave brands called 'Driven' and 'Rush'?

7. True or false – Derek Jeter appeared in more winning games than any other player in MLB history?

8. Which pitcher reached a record 105.1mph on the speed gun in a 2016 game against Baltimore?

9. The Yankees' #5 jersey is retired in honor of which great?

10. Which member of the Pro Football Hall of Fame made 71 appearances for the Yankees in 1989 and 1990?

11. Which Yankees bench coach wore a green army helmet during the 1999 ALDS after being struck by a Chuck Knoblaugh line drive in Game 1 of the series?

12. True or false – Former Yankee Dwight Gooden is the uncle of fellow former Yankee Gary Sheffield?

13. The longest streak of consecutive winning seasons in Yankees' history lasted how many years?

14. In what year did George Steinbrenner purchase the Yankees?

15. Steinbrenner purchased the team from which broadcasting corporation?

16. Billy Martin had how many separate spells managing the Yankees?

17. What is the name of the Major League Soccer team that plays its home games at Yankee Stadium?

18. Which two Yankees had over 200 hits during the 2002 season?

19. What was Mariano Rivera's career postseason ERA? a) 0.7 b) 0.8 c) 0.9

20. What was pitcher Whitey Ford's real first name? a) Albert b) Edward c) Henry

Quiz 10: Answers

1. 1995 2. Dennis Martinez 3. First 4. 20 years 5. Bobby Jones 6. Lou Gehrig 7. 14 times 8. Wade Boggs 9. Tampa Bay 10. 396 votes 11. Five 12. Byung-Hyun Kim 13. Five 14. Boston 15. Miami Marlins 16. Dave Winfield 17. True 18. Camden Yards 19. c) Sanderson 20. c) .310

Quiz 12: Firsts and Lasts

1. Which team did the Yankees defeat to claim their first World Series crown?

2. In what year did the team win that maiden World Championship?

3. In August 1938, Monte Pearson became the first pitcher to do what at Yankee Stadium?

4. On October 1, 2015, the Yankees became the first American League team to reach 10,000 regular season wins. Which team did they beat to record that historic win?

5. The Yankees suffered their first World Series loss to which team?

6. Which US President tossed the ceremonial first pitch in Game 3 of the 2001 World Series?

7. Who hit the last home run in the original Yankee Stadium?

8. What was special about the Yankees' game at the Philadelphia Athletics on 26 June 1939?

9. How did Elston Howard make history in an April 1954 game against Boston?

10. Which pair of Yankees switch-hitters became the first teammates in Major League history to hit home runs from both sides of the plate in the same game in a match up against Toronto in April 2000?

11. In an April 1973 game against Boston, the Yankees' Ron Blomberg became Major League Baseball's first what?

12. Which Yankees superstar recorded his first ever RBI after drawing a walk with the bases loaded in a June 2009 game against the Mets?

13. In March 2004, the Yankees played their first regular season games outside of North America. Which city hosted these games?

14. Which team did the Yankees face in this historic overseas series?

15. In what decade was the first night-game held at Yankee Stadium?

16. John Ganzel was the first player in franchise history to do what?

17. In a July 22, 2010 game against Kansas City, Derek Jeter became the last Yankee to do what at Yankee Stadium?

18. On June 12, 2008, which overseas star became the first Yankee to hit a grand slam on his birthday?

19. Which Yankee was the first Major League player to catch in over 100 games in 13 straight seasons? a) Yogi Berra b) Bill Dickey c) Jorge Posada

20. In what year did Lou Gehrig play his last game for the Yankees? a) 1939 b) 1940 c) 1941

Quiz 11: Answers

1. Dwight Gooden 2. Gary Sanchez 3. Nick Swisher 4. Once 5. John Miller 6. Derek Jeter 7. False (he's 4th on the list) 8. Aroldis Chapman 9. Joe DiMaggio 10. Deion Sanders 11. Don Zimmer 12. True 13. 39 years 14. 1973 15. CBS 16. Five 17. New York City FC 18. Alfonso Soriano and Bernie Williams 19. a) 0.7 ERA 20. b) Edward

Quiz 13: Pot Luck

1. Which Yankees great said, "Some people call October a time of pressure. I call it a time of character"?

2. Which Yankees catcher holds the AL record for hitting 100 HRs in the fewest number of games?

3. Which 46-year-old pitcher started on the opening day of the 1985 season, becoming the oldest player to do so in Yankees history?

4. Which Hall of Fame position player delivered a scoreless inning on his pitching debut for the Yankees against the Angels in August 1997?

5. What appeared on the team's uniform for the first time in April 1912?

6. Who holds the record for the most 'walk off' home runs in team history?

7. Which pair of Yankees pitchers both recorded their 200th career win in back-to-back games in April 2004?

8. Which Yankees left-hander threw a no-hitter against the Red Sox on July 4, 1983?

9. Who is the longest-serving captain in team history?

10. Which Yankee hit his 400th career home run in a May 2016 game against the White Sox?

11. Which fellow switch-hitter also slugged his 400th career home run just two months later in a July 2016 game vs. the Padres?

12. Which former Yankees pitcher has four sons all of whom have names that start with the letter K?

13. True or false - During 1919 Spring Training, Yankees outfielder Ping Bodie won a spaghetti eating contest against an ostrich?

14. Which knuckleball pitcher, who spent seven seasons with the Yankees in the 1960s, penned the classic baseball book 'Ball Four'?

15. Up to and including the end of the 2019 season, the Yankees had a perfect home record against which team?

16. Which Yankee's #44 jersey was retired in August 1993?

17. Which three-time Pro Bowl quarterback with football's Minnesota Vikings did the Yankees select in the 1995 MLB Draft?

18. Which relief pitcher struck out a Major League record eight straight batters in a 1981 game against the Angels?

19. What was the nickname of fiery former Yankee Kid Elberfeld? a) The Flame Out Kid b) The Red Hot Kid c) The Tabasco Kid

20. In 1998, the Yankees set a club record after winning how many games? a) 112 b) 113 c) 114

Quiz 12: Answers

1. New York Giants 2. 1923 3. Toss a no-hitter 4. Boston 5. New York Giants 6. George W. Bush 7. Jose Molina 8. It was their first ever night game 9. He became the Yankees' first black player 10. Jorge Posada and Bernie Williams 11. Designated Hitter 12. Mariano Rivera 13. Tokyo 14. Tampa Bay 15. 1940s 16. Hit a home run 17. Hit an inside the park home run 18. Hideki Matsui 19. b) Bill Dickey 20. a) 1939

Quiz 14: 1990s

1. The Yankees played their longest ever postseason game on October 4, 1995, defeating which team in 15 innings?

2. The Yankees defeated which team to win the 1996 World Series, the team's first championship in 18 years?

3. Which pitcher closed out the final game of the 1996 World Series to give the Yankees the championship?

4. Whom did Joe Torre succeed as the Yankees' manager in November 1995?

5. The Yankees swept which team 3-0 in the 1998 ALDS?

6. Which team did the Yankees defeat in the 1998 ALCS to reach the World Series?

7. The Yankees claimed the 1998 World Series after routing which team by 4 games to nil?

8. Which Yankees third baseman was named the MVP of the 1998 World Series?

9. Which Yankee won the AL batting title with an average of .359 in the strike-shortened 1994 season?

10. Who was the leadoff hitter on the all-conquering 1998 team?

11. Which Yankee won his only AL Batting Title in 1998 with a .339 average?

12. Which former Met hit 24 home runs in just 295 at bats during the 1998 season?

13. The Yankees made it back-to-back championships after sweeping which team in the 1999 World Series?

14. Who was the MVP of the 1999 World Series?

15. Who hit a famous walk-off homer to give the Yankees victory in Game 3 of the 1999 World Series?

16. True or false – During the 1999 postseason the Yankees posted an 11-1 record?

17. Who were the four Yankees pitchers to record at least 30 saves in a single season during the 1990s?

18. Who was the only Yankees batter to hit more than 40 home runs in a single season during the 1990s?

19. Between 1990 and 1999 the Yankees won how many AL East titles?
a) Three b) Four c) Five

20. The dominant 1998 Yankees won the AL East by how many games?
a) 18 b) 20 c) 22

Quiz 13: Answers

1. Reggie Jackson 2. Gary Sanchez 3. Phil Niekro 4. Wade Boggs 5. Pinstripes 6. Mickey Mantle 7. Mike Mussina and Kevin Brown 8. Dave Righetti 9. Derek Jeter 10. Carlos Beltran 11. Mark Teixeira 12. Roger Clemens 13. True 14. Jim Bouton 15. Chicago Cubs 16. Reggie Jackson 17. Daunte Culpepper 18. Ron Davis 19. c) The Tabasco Kid 20. c) 114

Quiz 15: Pot Luck

1. Which three Yankees each scored a Grand Slam in the same August 2011 game against Oakland?

2. Which Yankees pitcher famously threw part of a broken bat towards Mike Piazza in Game 2 of the 2000 World Series?

3. Which Yankees great was the first player to hit three home runs in a single World Series game?

4. Who hit a grand slam in the opening game of the 1998 World Series?

5. Which Yankee was the first full-time designated hitter to win the World Series MVP Award?

6. Which Kansas City batter was at the center of the controversy at the so-called 'Pine Tar Game' against the Yankees in July 1983?

7. Who led the Major Leagues in doubles in three-straight years in 1984, 1985 and 1986?

8. Do the Yankees have a winning or losing record in games played on Opening Day?

9. Which pitcher recorded 68 wins with an ERA of 3.90 and 557 strikeouts in his four seasons as a Yankee in 1997, 1998, 2002 and 2003?

10. The surgical procedure to reconstruct the ulnar collateral ligament is named after which former Yankees pitcher?

11. In a May 2015 game against Baltimore who became just the second right-handed Yankees pitcher to record 16 strikeouts in a single game?

12. Who was the first right-handed pitcher to manage that feat in June 1997?

13. Which legendary Yankee was married to Hollywood stars Dorothy Arnold and later Marilyn Monroe?

14. Alongside Roy Halladay, which Yankees pitcher is the only other member of the Baseball Hall of Fame from the state of Colorado?

15. Which former Yankee is the youngest player to be elected to the Japanese Baseball Hall of Fame?

16. Which broadcaster worked 5,060 games in a row before missing the Yankees' July 4, 2019 game against the Rays?

17. Which Heisman Trophy-winning quarterback turned NBA guard did the Yankees select in the 18th round of the 1994 MLB Draft?

18. 'Flash' was the nickname of which former Yankees relief pitcher?

19. Approximately how much did George Steinbrenner pay to purchase the Yankees? a) $1m b) $10m c) $100m

20. The longest winning streak in club history stretched to how many games? a) 18 b) 19 c) 20

Quiz 14: Answers

1. Seattle 2. Atlanta 3. John Wetteland 4. Buck Showalter 5. Texas 6. Cleveland 7. San Diego 8. Scott Brosius 9. Paul O'Neill 10. Chuck Knoblauch 11. Bernie Williams 12. Darryl Strawberry 13. Atlanta 14. Mariano Rivera 15. Chad Curtis 16. True 17. Dave Righetti, Steve Farr, John Wetteland and Mariano Rivera 18. Tino Martinez 19. a) Three 20. c) 22 games

Quiz 16: 2000s

1. The Yankees started the decade in style by winning their third successive world championship. Which club did they beat in the 2000 World Series?

2. The Yankees won the 2000 World Series in how many games?

3. Which team did the Yankees defeat in the 2000 ALCS?

4. Who was named the MVP of the 2000 World Series?

5. The Yankees reached the World Series again in 2001. Which team prevented them making it four world championships in a row?

6. The Yankees claimed the AL pennant in 2003 after which batter hit an 11th inning solo home run in the decisive Game 7 encounter against Boston?

7. Who was the Red Sox pitcher on the receiving end of that crucial Game 7 home run?

8. True or false – In a 2006 game against Toronto the Yankees scored at least one run in all nine innings?

9. During the 2000s, who was the only Yankee to steal 40 or more bases in a single season?

10. Which Taiwanese pitcher led the team in wins in 2006 and 2007?

11. Which Yankees pitcher was one out away from recording a perfect game in a September 2001 contest at Fenway Park against Boston?

12. Who succeeded Joe Torre as the team's manager in October 2007?

13. In a May 2002 game against the Twins, who became just the second Yankee in team history to hit a walk-off grand slam when his team was down by three runs?

14. Who were the three Yankees pitchers with 20 or more wins in a single season during the 2000s?

15. Who set a Yankees record with 696 at bats during the 2002 season?

16. Who appeared in a team record 163 regular season games in the 2003 season?

17. Which relief pitcher appeared in a record 86 games during the 2004 regular season?

18. Whose 204 hits in 2002 are the most by a Yankees switch-hitter in a single season?

19. Who was the only Yankee to win the AL MVP Award during the 2000s? a) Derek Jeter b) Hideki Matsui c) Alex Rodriguez

20. How many seasons did the Yankees fail to reach the playoffs during the 2000s? a) one b) two c) three

Quiz 15: Answers

1. Robinson Cano, Curtis Granderson and Russell Martin 2. Roger Clemens 3. Babe Ruth 4. Tino Martinez 5. Hideki Matsui 6. George Brett 7. Don Mattingly 8. Winning 9. David Wells 10. Tommy John 11. Michael Pineda 12. David Cone 13. Joe DiMaggio 14. Catfish Hunter 15. Hideki Matsui 16. John Sterling 17. Charlie Ward 18. Tom Gordon 19. b) $10m 20. b) 19 games

Quiz 17: Pot Luck

1. Whose six Grand Slams in 1987 are tied for the most in a single season in Major League history?

2. Derek Jeter recorded his 3,000th career hit in style, hitting which Cy Young Award-winning pitcher for a home run?

3. Which pitcher threw the first perfect game in team history?

4. Which Yankees outfielder was the unanimous choice for AL Rookie of the Year in 2017?

5. Babe Ruth hit the first home run in the first ever All-Star Game. In what year did that game take place?

6. Which Yankees outfielder's 10 triples led the AL in 2013?

7. True or false – The club has never lost more than 100 games in a single season?

8. In 2004, the Yankees became the first team in Major League history to lose a postseason series after taking a 3-0 lead. Which team beat them 4-3?

9. The trophy awarded to the outstanding rookie at Spring Training is named after which New York Times writer?

10. Who became just the fourth Yankee in team history to hit a grand slam on Opening Day after smashing Oakland's Barry Zito in April 2006?

11. Who are the three players, all Yankees, to have hit .500 or better and three home runs in the same World Series?

12. True or false – Clint and Todd Frazier are first cousins?

13. Which Yankees pinch-hitter hit two ninth inning grand slams in games against KC and Oakland in 1998?

14. True or false – Up to and including the 2019 season, the Yankees had 568 wins and 568 losses in games against Boston at Fenway Park?

15. In 1975, who became baseball's first modern era free agent?

16. The team's longest run of consecutive sub .500 seasons lasted how many years?

17. Mariano Rivera led the team in saves every year between 1997 and 2013 bar one. Who recorded the most saves in 2012?

18. True of false – The Yankees reached the postseason in all 12 years of Joe Torre's tenure as manager?

19. What is the most wins that the Yankees have recorded in a single decade? a) 960 b) 970 c) 980

20. In an August 1942 game against Philadelphia the Yankees set a Major League record (that still stands) by recording how many double plays? a) 6 b) 7 c) 8

Quiz 16: Answers

1. New York Mets 2. Five games 3. Seattle 4. Derek Jeter 5. Arizona 6. Aaron Boone 7. Tim Wakefield 8. True 9. Alfonso Soriano 10. Chien-Ming Wang 11. Mike Mussina 12. Joe Girardi 13. Jason Giambi 14. Roger Clemens, Mike Mussina and Andy Pettitte 15. Alfonso Soriano 16. Hideki Matsui 17. Paul Quantrill 18. Bernie Williams 19. c) Alex Rodriguez 20. a) One

Quiz 18: 2010s

1. Which team eliminated the Yankees in the 2019 ALCS?

2. Who was the Yankees' manager at the start of the 2010s?

3. Whose season batting average of .327 in 2019 was the best by a Yankees hitter during the 2010s?

4. Who were the three Yankees pitchers to strike out over 200 batters in a season during the decade?

5. True or false – The 2010s was the first decade the Yankees failed to win the World Series?

6. Who was the only Yankees pitcher to record a 20-win season during the 2010s?

7. Which Japanese starting pitcher led the team with the lowest ERA in 2012, 2013 and 2014?

8. Who were the four Yankees to win Gold Glove Awards in the 2010s?

9. Whose 27 home runs in 2018 are the most in a single season by a Yankees shortstop?

10. How many times did the Yankees reach the ALCS during the 2010s?

11. Which outfielder smashed 115 home runs in a four-year spell with the Yankees between 2010 and 2013?

12. Which 2004 first-round draft pick tied an MLB record against Toronto in September 2012 after striking out four batters in an inning?

13. Whose 135 strikeouts in 2014 are the most in a season by a Yankees relief pitcher in team history?

14. In an April 2015 loss to Boston, the Yankees played in the third longest game in team history. How many innings did the game last?

15. Which Boston infielder became the first player to hit for the cycle in a postseason game during Game 3 of the 2018 ALDS against the Yankees?

16. In December 2017, the Yankees acquired Giancarlo Stanton following a trade with which club?

17. Which Yankees pitcher's 14-3 win loss record in 2015 was the best winning percentage in the American League that year?

18. Who was the only Yankees batter to lead the AL in RBIs in a season during the 2010s?

19. The 2013 Yankees set a franchise record after going errorless in how many games? a) 100 b) 104 c) 108

20. How many AL East titles did the Yankees win during the 2010s? a) Three b) Four c) Five

Quiz 17: Answers

1. Don Mattingly 2. David Price 3. Don Larsen 4. Aaron Judge 5. 1933 6. Brett Gardner 7. False 8. Boston 9. James P. Dawson 10. Alex Rodriguez 11. Babe Ruth, Lou Gehrig and Hideki Matsui 12. False – They're unrelated 13. Darryl Strawberry 14. True 15. Catfish Hunter 16. Four years 17. Rafael Soriano 18. True 19. b) 970 games 20. b) 7

Quiz 19: Pot Luck

1. Whose 248 strikeouts in 1978 are the most in a single season by a Yankees pitcher?

2. Who holds the team record for the most career leadoff home runs?

3. Which one-handed pitcher tossed a no-hitter against the Indians in September 1993?

4. Which Yankees great was born Russell Earl O'Dey?

5. Which batter went a perfect 6 for 6 in a June 2008 win over the Royals?

6. In 1985, which two pitchers became just the second pair of brothers to play for the Yankees?

7. True or false – In his 14 years with the Yankees, Don Mattingly appeared in just one postseason series?

8. Who were the two New York pitchers to record 20 wins in a season during the 1980s?

9. In what year did the Yankees last record a losing record in the regular season?

10. Eight players, including pitcher Dellin Betances, were ejected from a fiery August 2017 game between the Yankees and which team?

11. 'Chasing the Dream: My Journey to the World Series' was the title of which legendary Yankee's 1997 autobiography?

12. Who marked his first at-bat with the Yankees on August 16, 2013 by hitting a home run against arch-rival Boston?

13. Prior to Aaron Judge, who was the last Yankees batter to hit 50 home runs in a season?

14. Which two-time World Series winner with the Yankees in the 1970s later became the team's manager, winning 224 games between 1986 & 1988?

15. What is the highest jersey number that has been retired by the Yankees?

16. That jersey number was retired to honor which player?

17. Who holds the record for the most wins as manager of the Yankees?

18. Former Yankee Didi Gregorious was born in which European country?

19. In the 1990s and 2000s the Yankees won how many AL East titles in a row? a) Seven b) Eight c) Nine

20. The 2014 Yankees set a franchise record after using how many players throughout the season? a) 50 b) 52 c) 54

Quiz 18: Answers

1. Houston 2. Joe Girardi 3. DJ LeMahieu 4. CC Sabathia, Michael Pineda and Luis Severino 5. False 6. CC Sabathia 7. Hiroki Kuroda 8. Mark Teixeira, Derek Jeter, Robinson Cano and Brett Gardner 9. Didi Gregorius 10. Four 11. Curtis Granderson 12. Phil Hughes 13. Dellin Betances 14. 19 innings 15. Brock Holt 16. Miami 17. Nathan Eovaldi 18. Curtis Granderson 19. c) 108 games 20. a) Three

Quiz 20: Hall of the Fame

1. Which Yankees great appears in the lyrics to Paul Simon's classic song 'Mrs Robinson'?

2. 'Man of Steal' was the nickname of which first ballot Hall of Famer who was with the Yankees from 1985 through to 1989?

3. Who holds the MLB record for the most postseason wins as a manager?

4. Which superstar won MVP honors in 1962 despite appearing on only 123 games that season?

5. In 2008, which 39-year-old Yankee became the oldest pitcher in MLB history to record his first 20-win season?

6. Which pitcher recorded 151 saves with an ERA of just 2.14 in a six-year spell with the Yankees in the late 70s and early 80s?

7. Which Yankees great was drafted by the NFL's Minnesota Vikings and the NBA's Atlanta Hawks?

8. Which Hall of Famer, who spent 2005 and 2006 with the Yankees, is second only to Nolan Ryan in 300-strikeout seasons?

9. Who steered the Yankees to seven World Series wins in his time as manager between 1949 and 1960?

10. Who spent a single season as manager of the Yankees in 1964 then returned to the club 20 years later for a second spell in charge?

11. Which manager, who led the Atlanta Braves to 14 straight division titles, spent 10 years with the Yankees organization as a player, minor league manager and major league coach?

12. 'Pudge' was the nickname of which catcher who enjoyed a brief stint with the Yankees in 2008?

13. Which superstitious Hall of Famer would famously eat chicken before every game he played?

14. Reggie Jackson was the first player in MLB history to hit 100 home runs with three different clubs. The Yankees were one. Who were the other two?

15. Which veteran Hall of Fame pitcher registered his 300th career win during a brief spell with the Yankees in 1985?

16. What was Catfish Hunter's given first name?

17. Which Hall of Fame pitcher was on the mound during the ninth inning of the infamous 'Pine Tar Game'?

18. In 1983, which Yankees great appeared on a US 20c postage stamp?

19. Which catcher made 1,789 appearances for the Yankees between 1928 and 1946?

20. What was the nickname of Hall of Famer Frank Baker? a) Big Bash b) Home Run c) Lightning

Quiz 19: Answers

1. Ron Guidry 2. Derek Jeter 3. Jim Abbott 4. Bucky Dent 5. Johnny Damon 6. Phil & Joe Niekro 7. True 8. Tommy John & Ron Guidry 9. 1992 10. Detroit 11. Joe Torre 12. Mark Reynolds 13. Alex Rodriguez 14. Lou Piniella 15. #51 16. Bernie Williams 17. Joe McCarthy 18. The Netherlands 19. c) Nine 20. c) 54 players

Quiz 21: Pot Luck

1. Up to the start of the 2020 season the Yankees had won how many World Championships?

2. Who famously completed the so-called 'Flip Play' in Game 3 of the 2001 ALDS against Oakland?

3. The player thrown out at the plate during the 'Flip Play' went on to play for the Yankees from 2002 to 2008. Who was he?

4. Who are the three Yankees to have won the World Series as both a player and manager?

5. Which Yankees pitcher created a Major League record after committing three errors on a single play against the Brewers in July 1988?

6. In 2005, who set the team record for giving up the most home runs by a left-handed pitcher in a single season?

7. Who is the only Yankee to have hit two HRs in his first two plate appearances?

8. Whom did Aaron Boone succeed as Yankees manager?

9. Which Yankees pitcher was immortalized in a 1976 song by Bob Dylan?

10. Which Yankees great and crossword lover appeared in a 2006 documentary on the subject called 'Wordplay'?

11. Which former Yankee penned a 2009 children's book called 'All You Can Be: Dream It, Draw It, Become It!'?

12. In June 2019, which Yankee became the first MLB player to hit a regular season home run in Europe?

13. Who is the tallest player to wear the famous Yankees pinstripes in team history?

14. Which quartet of Yankees were known collectively as the 'Core Four'?

15. What name is missing? Bucky Dent, ????, Buck Showalter, Joe Torre

16. The Yankees' #8 jersey was retired to honor which team great?

17. Which former Yankees relief pitcher appears in the title of novel by horror writer Stephen King?

18. Alex Rodriguez and which Red Sox catcher were both ejected following a brawl in a July 2004 game at Fenway Park?

19. Who holds the team record for the most stolen bases in a single season? a) Brett Gardner b) Rickey Henderson c) Derek Jeter

20. How many bases did he steal to set that record? a) 89 b) 91 c) 93

Quiz 20: Answers

1. Joe DiMaggio 2. Rickey Henderson 3. Joe Torre 4. Mickey Mantle 5. Mike Mussina 6. Goose Gossage 7. Dave Winfield 8. Randy Johnson 9. Casey Stengel 10. Yogi Berra 11. Bobby Cox 12. Ivan Rodriguez 13. Wade Boggs 14. A's and Angels 15. Phil Niekro 16. James 17. Goose Gossage 18. Babe Ruth 19. Bill Dickey 20. b) Home Run

Quiz 22: Nicknames

Match the nickname to the current or former Yankee.

1. Godzilla   A. George Steinbrenner

2. Moose   B. Wade Boggs

3. Boomer   C. Lou Gehrig

4. Chairman of the Board   D. Mike Mussina

5. Sandman   E. Hideki Matsui

6. Mr. October   F. Derek Jeter

7. The Boss   G. Randy Johnson

8. Scooter   H. Adrian Hernandez

9. The Commerce Comet   I. Reggie Jackson

10. The Iron Horse   J. David Wells

11. The Sultan of Swat   K. Bernie Williams

12. The Chicken Man   L. George Stirnweiss

13. Bambi   M. Joe DiMaggio

14. All Rise   N. Mariano Rivera

15. Captain Clutch   O. Phil Rizzuto

16. El Duquecito   P. Mickey Mantle

17. Snuffy	Q. Babe Ruth
18. Knucksie	R. Aaron Judge
19. The Yankee Clipper	S. Phil Niekro
20. The Big Unit	T. Whitey Ford

Quiz 21: Answers

1. 27 Championships 2. Derek Jeter 3. Jason Giambi 4. Billy Martin, Ralph Houk and Joe Girardi 5. Tommy John 6. Randy Johnson 7. Cody Ransom 8. Joe Girardi 9. Catfish Hunter 10. Mike Mussina 11. Curtis Granderson 12. Aaron Hicks 13. Randy Johnson 14. Derek Jeter, Andy Pettitte, Mariano Rivera and Jorge Posada 15. Stump Merrill 16. Yogi Berra 17. Tom Gordon 18. Jason Varitek 19. b) Rickey Henderson 20. c) 93

Quiz 23: Pot Luck

1. Who is the Yankees' all-time leader in stolen bases?

2. Who are the two Yankees to have won the AL batting triple crown?

3. Which number nine hitter struck a three-run homer in the Yankees' 5-4 win over the Red Sox in a 1978 one-game tie-breaker playoff?

4. Which Yankee holds the Major League record for the most walks as a rookie?

5. Who was the first Japanese player to be named the World Series MVP?

6. Who was the only Yankees pitcher to win the AL Cy Young Award during the 2000s?

7. Which Yankees legend co-wrote a best-selling autobiography with his wife called 'The Beauty of Love: A Memoir of Miracles, Hope, and Healing'?

8. In a May 2018 game against the Indians, which 21-year-old became the youngest Yankee to hit a home run since the 1960s?

9. Which team overturned a 2-0 deficit to defeat the Yankees in five games in the 1995 ALDS?

10. Which long-time Atlanta Brave hit a home run in his first at-bat as a Yankee in an April 5, 2011 game against the Twins?

11. The Yankees were involved in an infamous 1998 bench-clearing brawl with which team after Tino Martinez was hit by a pitch?

12. Which closer, who later went on to play for the Yankees, received an eight-game ban for causing the brawl?

13. Why is Jeffrey Maier an important name in Yankees folklore?

14. In 1977, who became just the second relief pitcher to win the Cy Young Award?

15. The Yankees reached the 1976 World Series after which batter hit a walk-off home run to defeat the Royals in Game 5 of the ALCS?

16. Prior to Aaron Boone, who was the last Yankees manager to have never previously managed a Major League ball club?

17. What job did George Costanza have with the Yankees in the classic TV comedy 'Seinfeld'?

18. The longest game in team history took place in 1967. How many innings did it last?

19. Which team did the Yankees face in this marathon encounter? a) Boston b) Cleveland c) Detroit

20. What was Babe Ruth's real first name? a) John b) Paul c) George

Quiz 22: Answers

1. E Hideki Matsui 2. D Mike Mussina 3. J David Wells 4. T Whitey Ford. 5. N Mariano Rivera 6. I Reggie Jackson 7. A George Steinbrenner 8. O Phil Rizzuto 9. P Mickey Mantle 10. C Lou Gehrig 11. Q Babe Ruth 12. B Wade Boggs 13. K Bernie Williams 14. R Aaron Judge 15. F Derek Jeter 16. H Adrian Hernandez 17. L George Stirnweiss 18. S Phil Niekro 19. M Joe DiMaggio 20. G Randy Johnson

Quiz 24: Anagrams

Re-arrange the letters to make the name of a current or former Yankee.

1. Herb Tuba

2. Jaguar Node

3. Tree Jerked

4. Arrive Romania

5. Adore Spa Jog

6. Serbia Wine Mill

7. Jocks Agreeing

8. Root Jeer

9. I Hike Stadium

10. Patty Tide Ten

11. Mink I Assume

12. Long Intro Canasta

13. Carbon Onions

14. Your Grind

15. A Milky Cement

16. My Tan Gold Tin

17. Locker Washtub

18. Deify Throw

19. Noon Solo Safari

20. Mirrors Age

Quiz 23: Answers

1. Derek Jeter 2. Lou Gehrig and Micky Mantle 3. Bucky Dent 4. Aaron
Judge 5. Hideki Matsui 6. Roger Clemens 7. Jorge Posada 8. Gleyber
Torres 9. Seattle 10. Andruw Jones 11. Baltimore 12. Armando Benitez
13. The 12-year-old leaned over the wall to catch a Derek Jeter 'Home
Run' in Game 1 of the 1996 ALCS 14. Sparky Lyle 15. Chris Chambliss 16.
Buck Showalter 17. Assistant to the Traveling Secretary 18. 22 innings
19. c) Detroit 20. c) George

Quiz 25: Pot Luck

1. Mariano Rivera would head to the mound to the accompaniment of which song by US rockers Metallica?

2. Which infielder's 47 doubles in 2018 were the second most by a rookie in Major League history?

3. In 1975, which right-fielder became the first player in Yankees history with 30 home runs and 30 stolen bases in the same season?

4. Who blasted three home runs in Game 6 of the 1977 World Series to give the Yankees their first championship since 1962?

5. Which team did the Yankees defeat to win that 1977 World Series?

6. In 2017, which Yankees batter became the first rookie to win the Home Run Derby outright?

7. Which legendary Yankee was named an All-Star every year from 1948 through to 1962?

8. What do the letters DJ stand for in the name of DJ LeMahieu?

9. Which five-time All-Star pitcher from the 60s and 70s never won the World Series as a player but won four Championships as the Yankees' pitching coach in the late 1990s and early 2000s?

10. Who was on the mound for the Yankees to deliver the final out in the famous 1978 playoff win against Boston?

11. In the 1961 World Series, which left-handed pitcher set a record after going 33 2/3 innings without giving up a run?

12. Which Yankees great was the previously the holder of the that scoreless streak record?

13. Who is the only Yankee to have hit two postseason walk-off home runs?

14. Which Yankee holds the record for the most postseason appearances in MLB history?

15. Which Hollywood superstar played Lou Gehrig in the 1942 movie 'The Pride of the Yankees'?

16. 'Donnie Baseball' was the nickname of which popular Yankee?

17. A reporter called Fred Lieb is credited with penning what famous nickname for the original Yankee Stadium?

18. Who has been the Yankees' general manager since 1998?

19. What is Didi Gregorius's real first name? a) Diederick b) Mariekson c) Willem

20. How many postseason saves did Mariano Rivera record during his stellar career? a) 41 b) 42 c) 43

Quiz 24: Answers

1. Babe Ruth 2. Aaron Judge 3. Derek Jeter 4. Mariano Rivera 5. Jorge Posada 6. Bernie Williams 7. Reggie Jackson 8. Joe Torre 9. Hideki Matsui 10. Andy Pettitte 11. Mike Mussina 12. Giancarlo Stanton 13. Robinson Cano 14. Ron Guidry 15. Mickey Mantle 16. Don Mattingly 17. Buck Showalter 18. Whitey Ford 19. Alfonso Soriano 20. Roger Maris

Made in the USA
Middletown, DE
11 January 2024

47694708R00035